The Stations of the Cross

With Pope John Paul II

The Stations of the Cross

With Pope John Paul II

Joseph M. Champlin

Liguori
ONE LIGUORI DRIVE
LIGUORI MO 63057-9999

Imprimi Potest:
James Shea, CSsR
Provincial, St. Louis Province
The Redemptorists

Imprimatur:
+ Edward J. O'Donnell, DD
Auxiliary Bishop, Archdiocese of St. Louis

ISBN 978-0-89243-679-8

16 15 14 13 12 / 23 22 21 20 19

Liguori Publications, a nonprofit corporation, is an apostolate of the Redemptorists. To learn more about the Redemptorists, visit *Redemptorists.com*.

To order, call 800-325-9521
www.liguori.org

Cover design and illustrations by Grady Gunter
Photograph by Catholic News Service

Joannes Paulus PP. II

On Good Friday, 1991, Pope John Paul II, according to long-standing papal tradition, led a crowd of people at the Roman Colosseum through the Stations of the Cross. However, he changed the format, altering the fourteen stations and adding a fifteenth. Some of the traditional ones were kept, while others were dropped and new ones were inserted. All of the stations the Holy Father used had as their basis incidents recorded in the gospels.

In this booklet, I have adapted, for both public and private use, Pope John Paul II's version of this venerable devotion. Starting with the passion narratives as found in the Gospels of Mark, Luke, and John, I devised the format, composed the reflections following each gospel excerpt, and selected portions from different Psalms as prayer responses to each station. These include verses from Psalms 6 (stations 1-4), 130 (5-7), 32 (8), 38 (9-10), 51 (11), 143 (12), 22 (13), 62 (14), and 146 (15).

When parishes or groups celebrate these stations publicly, they may be done in the context of Exposition and Benediction of the Blessed Sacrament. The Eucharist is at once a memorial of the Lord's passion and death as well as the Real Presence of the risen Christ in our midst. Integration of the stations with a eucharistic devotional service seems, therefore, theologically sound, liturgically appropriate, and pastorally wise. You may wish to refer to *Holy Communion and Worship of the Eucharist Outside Mass*, numbers 79–100, for further guidelines and directives concerning eucharistic Exposition and Benediction, as well as an outline of the rite itself.

In parish churches or other locations that have stations which depict the more traditional version of this devotion, the illustrations in this booklet should help participants visualize the "new" stations according to the pattern adopted by Pope John Paul II. The altar or tabernacle might be an appropriate place to mark the fifteenth station.

Our parish staff at St. Joseph's "On-the-Hill" in Camillus, New York, compiled the original booklet on which this one is based. My colleague, Father John Broderick, composed a hymn with a verse for each station to be sung to the melody of the ancient and customary "*Stabat Mater.*" The religious education staff—Betty Drotar, Sister Gratia Eallonardo, O.S.F., and Kristen Huck-Morey—

reviewed the texts, made suggestions, and enlisted the aid of young parishioners in sketching pictures for the stations that appeared in the original booklet.

My thanks to all of them and to Rev. Ron Krisman of the Secretariat for Liturgy, National Conference of Catholic Bishops, who provided us with essential information at the beginning of our project.

It is my hope that this new, biblically rich approach will help users at all times, but most especially during their Lenten journeys when they seek to die with Christ in the hope of rising with him on Easter Sunday.

FATHER JOSEPH M. CHAMPLIN
PASTOR, ST. JOSEPH'S CHURCH
CAMILLUS, NEW YORK

"If any want to become my
followers, let them
deny themselves and take
up their cross and follow me..."

The Agony of Jesus in the Garden of Olives

Leader: We adore you, O Christ, and we praise you.
(Genuflect)

All: Because by your holy cross you have saved the world.
(Stand)

Reader: Then they came to a place named Gethsemane, and he said to his disciples, "Sit here while I pray." He took with him Peter, James, and John, and began to be troubled and distressed. Then he said to them, "My soul is sorrowful even to death. Remain here and keep watch." He advanced a little and fell to the ground and prayed that if it were possible the hour might pass by him; he said, "Abba, Father, all things are possible to you. Take this cup away from me, but not what I will but what you will."

Mark 14:32-36

(Kneel)

Leader: Jesus felt sorrow and dread over what lay ahead of him. He prayed for the burden to be lifted and the cross to be removed, but only if the Father willed it so. When Christ saw clearly that he must drink of the bitter cup, then our Lord totally accepted his future. "Not my will, but thine be done." His example teaches us how to pray at all times, especially in the midst of our own crosses and cups of suffering.

   All: Do not reprove me in your anger, LORD,
      nor punish me in your wrath.
      Have pity on me, LORD, for I am weak;
      heal me, LORD, for my bones are shuddering.
      In utter terror is my soul.

Psalm 6:2-4a

(Stand)

All sing:

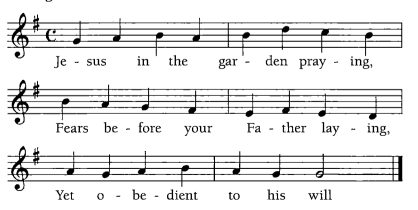

Je - sus in the gar - den pray - ing,

Fears be - fore your Fa - ther lay - ing,

Yet o - be - dient to his will

The Second Station

The Betrayal and Arrest of Jesus

Leader: We adore you, O Christ, and we praise you.
(Genuflect)

All: Because by your holy cross you have saved the world.
(Stand)

Reader: Judas, one of the Twelve, arrived, accompanied by a crowd with swords and clubs who had come from the chief priests, the scribes, and the elders. His betrayer had arranged a signal with them, saying, "The man I shall kiss is the one; arrest him and lead him away securely." He came and immediately went over to him and said, "Rabbi." And he kissed him. At this they laid hands on him and arrested him.

Mark 14:43-46

(Kneel)

Leader: Rejection always hurts. It tears at our self-esteem and leaves us doubting our own worth. Even the turning down of a simple invitation can wound us. Betrayal, especially by a friend, hurts even more. Jesus had prayed all night before selecting his twelve apostles, including Judas. Judas had also been his companion for three years, hearing the Lord's words and observing his miraculous deeds. Now he betrays his savior with a kiss, and for but a few dollars. Remembering Jesus' hurt and pain in the garden can help us deal with those times when we feel rejected and betrayed.

All: Turn back, LORD, rescue my soul
save me because of your mercy.
For in death there is no remembrance of you.
Who praises you in Sheol?

Psalm 6:5-6

(Stand)

All sing:

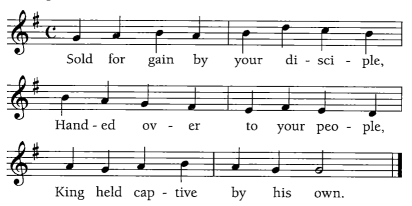

Sold for gain by your di - sci - ple,

Hand - ed ov - er to your peo - ple,

King held cap - tive by his own.

The Sanhedrin Condemns Jesus

Leader: We adore you, O Christ, and we praise you.
(*Genuflect*)

All: Because by your holy cross you have saved the world.
(*Stand*)

Reader: The chief priests and the entire Sanhedrin kept trying to obtain testimony against Jesus in order to put him to death, but they found none....The high priest rose before the assembly and questioned Jesus, saying, "Have you no answer? What are these men testifying against you?" But he was silent and answered nothing. Again the high priest asked him and said to him, "Are you the Messiah, the son of the Blessed One?" Then Jesus answered, "I am; and 'you will see the Son of Man seated at the right hand of the Power and coming with the clouds of heaven.' At that the high priest tore his garments and said, "What further need have we of witnesses?"

Mark 14:55,60-63

(*Kneel*)

Leader: Envy and jealousy can be like cancerous diseases within us. They spread throughout our whole being, leading to uncharitable conversations, false accusations, and other destructive actions. We see all of this played out among the religious leaders of Jesus' time as they condemn Christ without basis. Our Lord offers a model for us: he did not defend himself, but remained silent before the false accusations. Jesus did, however, assert himself, speaking the truth regardless of the cost.

All: I am wearied with sighing;
all night long I drench my bed with tears;
I soak my couch with weeping.
My eyes are dimmed with sorrow,
worn out because of all my foes.

Psalm 6:7-8

(Stand)

All sing:

Judge of all, you stand con - vict - ed,

Of the sin that we've com - mit - ted.

All for love you bear our guilt.

The Fourth Station

Peter Denies Jesus

Leader: We adore you, O Christ, and we praise you.
(Genuflect)

All: Because by your holy cross you have saved the world.
(Stand)

Reader: While Peter was below in the courtyard, one of the high priest's maids came along. Seeing Peter warming himself, she looked intently at him and said, "You too were with the Nazarene, Jesus." But he denied it saying, "I neither know nor understand what you are talking about." So he went out into the outer court. [Then the cock crowed.] The maid saw him and began again to say to the bystanders, "This man is one of them." Once again he denied it. A little later the bystanders said to Peter once more, "Surely you are one of them; for you too are a Galilean." He began to curse and to swear, "I do not know this man about whom you are talking." And immediately a cock crowed a second time. Then Peter remembered the word that Jesus had said to him, "Before the cock crows twice you will deny me three times." He broke down and wept.

Mark 14:66-72

(Kneel)

Leader: All of us are like Peter to an extent, willing but weak. We make resolutions, but don't keep them. We try to start a new life, but slip back again into a way of darkness.

Yet weak as Peter was—not only at Jesus' trial but at other times as well—he truly loved Jesus. In fact, it was his love that repeatedly set him up for failure. All of Christ's other followers ran away after his arrest. Peter, however, followed along into the courtyard, only there to see his weakness take over. Almost immediately, he wept because of what he had done. A few short days afterward, Jesus would take this weak but loving follower and make him head of the Church, supplying him with divine strength to overcome his human weakness.

All: The Lord has heard the sound of my weeping.
The Lord has heard my plea;
the Lord will receive my prayer.
My foes will all be disgraced and will shudder greatly;
they will turn back in sudden disgrace.

Psalm 6:9-11

(Stand)

All sing:

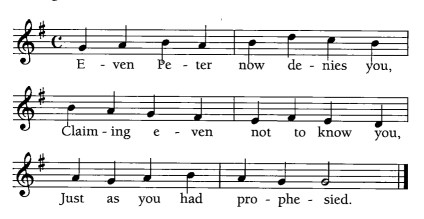

E - ven Pe - ter now de - nies you,

Claim - ing e - ven not to know you,

Just as you had pro - phe - sied.

The Fifth Station

Pilate Condemns Jesus to the Cross

Leader: We adore you, O Christ, and we praise you.
(Genuflect)

All: Because by your holy cross you have saved the world.
(Stand)

Reader: As soon as morning came, the chief priests with the elders and the scribes, that is, the whole Sanhedrin, held a council. They bound Jesus, led him away, and handed him over to Pilate....Now on the occasion of the feast he used to release to them one prisoner whom they requested. A man called Barabbas was then in prison along with the rebels who had committed murder in a rebellion. The crowd came forward and began to ask him to do for them as he was accustomed. Pilate answered, "Do you want me to release to you the king of the Jews?" For he knew that it was out of envy that the chief priests had handed him over. But the chief priests stirred up the crowd to have him release Barabbas for them instead. Pilate again said to them in reply, "Then what [do you want] me to do with [the man you call] the king of the Jews?" They shouted again, "Crucify him." Pilate said to them, "Why? What evil has he done?" They only shouted the louder, "Crucify him." So Pilate, wishing to satisfy the crowd, released Barabbas to them and, after he had Jesus scourged, handed him over to be crucified.

Mark 15:1,6-15

(Kneel)

Leader: Pilate seemed anxious to release Jesus, almost looking for a way to do so. But the crowd would not allow that. Pilate capitulated, fearing for his future and lacking the courage to do what was right. We have, on occasion, acted similarly.

All: Out of depths I call to you, LORD;
Lord, hear my cry!
May your ears be attentive
to my cry for mercy.
If you, LORD, keep account of sins,
Lord, who can stand?
But with you is forgiveness
and so you are revered.

Psalm 130:1-4

(Stand)

All sing:

To the rul - ing pow'rs de - liv - ered,

By the crowd your ver - dict ren - dered,

Shunned by those you came to save.

19

Jesus Is Scourged and Crowned With Thorns

Leader: We adore you, O Christ, and we praise you.
(Genuflect)

All: Because by your holy cross you have saved the world.
(Stand)

Reader: Then Pilate took Jesus and had him scourged. And the soldiers wove a crown out of thorns and placed it on his head, and clothed him in a purple cloak, and they came to him and said, "Hail, King of the Jews!" And they struck him repeatedly.

John 19:1-3

(Kneel)

Leader: Pilate had Jesus scourged—a truly cruel punishment. He was probably stripped to the waist and made to bend over a short pillar. Then he was lashed several dozen times with a whip, the first few of those strokes cutting open the skin on his back. After the scourging, a wooden band, or crown, of long, sharp thorns was pressed into his scalp. The pain had to be excruciating. When our own head hurts or we suffer some other bodily pain, it would do well for us to follow the advice in the Letter to the Hebrews: "Let us...[keep] our eyes fixed on Jesus...For the sake of the joy that lay before him he endured the cross..." (Hebrews 12:1-2).

All: I wait for the LORD,
my soul waits
and I hope for his word.
My soul looks for the Lord
more than sentinels for daybreak.

Psalm 130:5-6a

(Stand)

All sing:

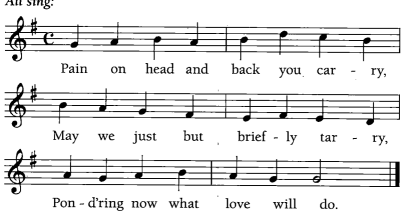

Pain on head and back you carry,

May we just but brief - ly tar - ry,

Pon - d'ring now what love will do.

Jesus Is Mocked by the Soldiers and Given His Cross

Leader: We adore you, O Christ, and we praise you.
(Genuflect)

All: Because by your holy cross you have saved the world.
(Stand)

Reader: The soldiers led him away inside the palace, that is, the praetorium, and assembled the whole cohort....They began to salute him...and kept striking his head with a reed and spitting upon him. They knelt before him in homage. And when they had mocked him, they stripped him of the purple cloak, dressed him in his own clothes, and led him out to crucify him.

Mark 15:16,18a,19-20

(Kneel)

Leader: Jesus is King of Kings and Lord of Lords. He deserves our praise and reverence. Yet the soldiers placed upon him a dirty cloak instead of a royal garment. They handed him a thin reed instead of the golden staff used by kings. Through all this humiliation, Jesus remained silent. How different with us. Though not as pure or as important as Christ, we nevertheless become angry and defensive when someone attacks or criticizes us in any way.

All: More than sentinels for daybreak,
   let Israel hope in the LORD,
   For with the LORD is mercy,
   with him is plenteous redemption,
   And he will redeem Israel
   from all its sins.

Psalm 130:6b-8

(Stand)

All sing:

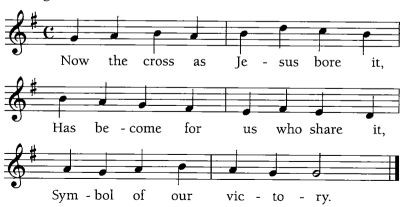

Now the cross as Je - sus bore it,

Has be - come for us who share it,

Sym - bol of our vic - to - ry.

Simon the Cyrenian Helps Jesus Carry His Cross

Leader: We adore you, O Christ, and we praise you.
(*Genuflect*)

All: Because by your holy cross you have saved the world.
(*Stand*)

Reader: They pressed into service a passer-by, Simon, a Cyrenian, who was coming in from the country, the father of Alexander and Rufus, to carry his cross.

Mark 15:21

(*Kneel*)

Leader: Those in charge of Jesus' crucifixion compelled Simon of Cyrene to help carry the Lord's cross. He did not volunteer or willingly accept the task, but that is no surprise. Simon was only passing by and presumably knew little about Christ. We, on the other hand, do know Jesus. And we have heard his words about the necessity of taking up our own crosses each day and walking in his footsteps. What is our response? Must we be pressed to carry our crosses, be they big or small, or do we accept them willingly?

All: Because I kept silent, my bones wasted away;
I groaned all day long.
For day and night your hand was heavy upon me;
my strength withered as in dry summer heat.
Then I declared my sin to you;
my guilt I did not hide.
I said, "I confess my transgression to the LORD,"
and you took away the guilt of my sin.

Psalm 32:3-5

(Stand)

All sing:

Si - mon bears with hes - i - ta - tion
Glo - rious sign of our sal - va - tion,
That which we should bear with joy.

The Ninth Station

Jesus Meets the Women of Jerusalem

Leader: We adore you, O Christ, and we praise you.
  (Genuflect)

All: Because by your holy cross you have saved the world.
  (Stand)

Reader: A large crowd of people followed Jesus, including many women who mourned and lamented him. Jesus turned to them and said, "Daughters of Jerusalem, do not weep for me; weep instead for yourselves and for your children."

Luke 23:27-28

  (Kneel)

Leader: Compassion means, literally, to suffer with someone. Empathy means to feel with them. These women displayed both qualities as they accompanied Jesus, so bruised and disfigured, on this sorrowful journey through the streets of Jerusalem. We imitate their example when we listen with love to another's troubles, hold another's hand by a hospital bed, or embrace another who is grieving.

All: LORD, do not punish me in your anger;
  in your wrath do not chastise me!
  Your arrows have sunk deep in me;
  your hand has come down upon me.

Psalm 38:2-3

  (Stand)

All sing:

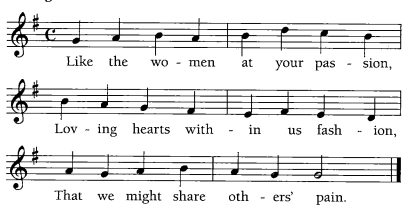

Like the wo - men at your pas - sion,

Lov - ing hearts with - in us fash - ion,

That we might share oth - ers' pain.

The Tenth Station

Jesus Is Crucified

Leader: We adore you, O Christ, and we praise you.
(Genuflect)

All: Because by your holy cross you have saved the world.
(Stand)

Reader: They brought him to the place of Golgotha (which is translated Place of the Skull). They gave him wine drugged with myrrh, but he did not take it. Then they crucified him and divided his garments by casting lots for them to see what each should take.

Mark 15:22-24

(Kneel)

Leader: First they drove nails through his hands and feet. Then they raised him on the cross, where he hung painfully for three hours—an example of patience for all to study. Pope John XXIII had a crucifix on his bedroom wall. He prayed in front of it before retiring, upon arising, and whenever cares awakened him during the night. "A cross," he said, "is the primary symbol of God's love for us."

All: My LORD, my deepest yearning is before you;
my groaning is not hidden from you.
My heart shudders, my strength forsakes me;
the very light of my eyes has failed.
Friends and companions shun my disease;
my neighbors stand far off.

Psalm 38:10-12

(Stand)

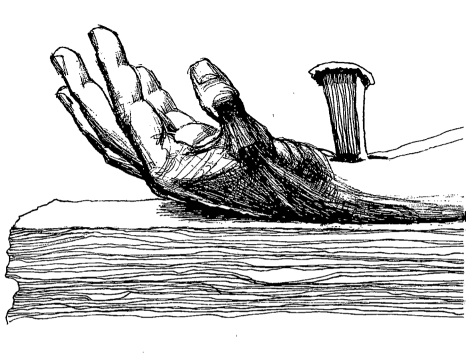

All sing:

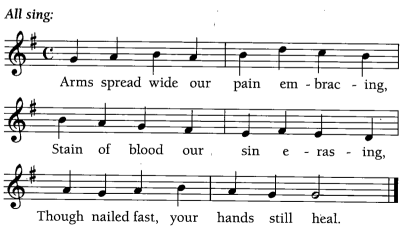

Arms spread wide our pain em - brac - ing,

Stain of blood our sin e - ras - ing,

Though nailed fast, your hands still heal.

The Eleventh Station

Jesus Promises Paradise to the Penitent Criminal

Leader: We adore you, O Christ, and we praise you.
(Genuflect)

All: Because by your holy cross you have saved the world.
(Stand)

Reader: When they came to the place called the Skull, they crucified him and the criminals there, one on his right, the other on his left....Now one of the criminals hanging there reviled Jesus, saying, "Are you not the Messiah? Save yourself and us." The other, however, rebuking him, said in reply, "Have you no fear of God, for you are subject to the same condemnation? And indeed, we have been condemned justly, for the sentence we received corresponds to our crimes, but this man has done nothing criminal." Then he said, "Jesus, remember me when you come into your kingdom." He replied to him, "Amen, I say to you, today you will be with me in Paradise."

Luke 23:33,39-43

(Kneel)

Leader: One criminal said "no" to Christ, the other "yes." To his penitent companion on Calvary, Jesus promised immediate forgiveness and entrance into heaven. When we doubt God's willingness to forgive us, when we keep punishing ourselves for past mistakes, when we dread the thought of standing before the pure Christ with our not-so-pure lives, we might recall this scene on the cross and draw hope from it.

All: Have mercy on me, God, in accord with your merciful love;
in your abundant compassion blot out my transgressions.
Thoroughly wash away my guilt;
and from my sin cleanse me....
You will let me hear gladness and joy;
the bones you have crushed will rejoice.

Psalm 51:3-4,10

(Stand)

All sing:

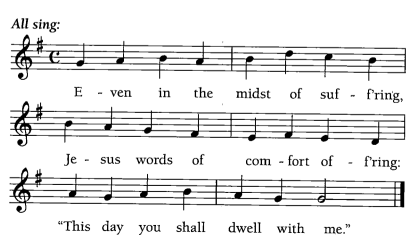

E - ven in the midst of suf - f'ring,

Je - sus words of com - fort of - f'ring:

"This day you shall dwell with me."

Jesus Speaks to His Mother and to His Disciple

Leader: We adore you, O Christ, and we praise you.
  (Genuflect)

All: Because by your holy cross you have saved the world.
  (Stand)

Reader: Standing by the cross of Jesus were his mother and his mother's sister, Mary the wife of Clopas, and Mary of Magdala. When Jesus saw his mother and the disciple there whom he loved, he said to his mother, "Woman, behold, your son." Then he said to the disciple, "Behold, your mother." And from that hour the disciple took her into his home.

John 19:25-27

  (Kneel)

Leader: With these words, Jesus gives his mother to us, making her our mother as well. Mary becomes the Mother of the Church. We can rely upon her for help and look to her as a model. Here, she stands at the foot of the cross, offering her son for us and for the whole world. She reminds us that if we unite our sufferings, both large and small, with her son on the cross and with her at the foot of the cross, we will share in Christ's work of bringing grace and blessings to others.

  All: Hasten to answer me, LORD;
       for my spirit fails me.
       Do not hide your face from me,
       lest I become like those descending to the pit.

In the morning let me hear of your mercy,
for in you I trust.
Show me the path I should walk,
for I entrust my life to you.   *Psalm 143:7-8*

(Stand)

All sing:

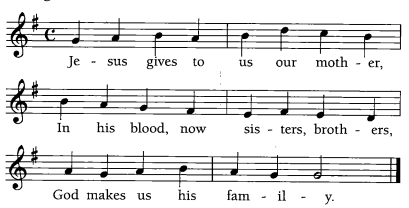

Je - sus gives to us our moth - er,

In his blood, now sis - ters, broth - ers,

God makes us his fam - il - y.

The Thirteenth Station

Jesus Dies on the Cross

Leader: We adore you, O Christ, and we praise you.
(Genuflect)

All: Because by your holy cross you have saved the world.
(Stand)

Reader: At noon darkness came over the whole land until three in the afternoon. And at three o'clock Jesus cried out in a loud voice, *"Eloi, Eloi, lema sabachtani?"* which is translated, "My God, my God, why have you forsaken me?" Some of the bystanders who heard it said, "Look, he is calling Elijah." One of them ran, soaked a sponge with wine, put it on a reed, and gave it to him to drink, saying, "Wait, let us see if Elijah comes to take him down." Jesus gave a loud cry and breathed his last.

Mark 15:33-37

(Kneel)

Leader: Jesus, as a faithful Jew, would have prayed the Psalms regularly. It is no surprise, then, that these words from Psalm 22 are on his lips during the intense agony of his last moments. While this cry might seem to be a sign of despair or hopelessness, it reveals, rather, the depth of his anguish and the intensity of his pain. Shortly afterward, he surrenders totally to his Father's will—"Father, into your hands, I commend my spirit." We might wish to follow Christ's example, letting these words be the last on our lips as we wait each night for sleep to come, sleep which is a symbol of our own eventual death.

All: My God, my God, why have you abandoned me?
Why so far from my call for help,
from my cries of anguish?

My God, I call by day, but you do not answer;
by night, but I have no relief.

Psalm 22:2-3

(Stand)

All sing:

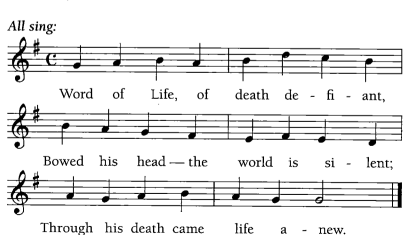

Word of Life, of death de - fi - ant,

Bowed his head — the world is si - lent;

Through his death came life a - new.

35

The Fourteenth Station

The Burial of Jesus

Leader: We adore you, O Christ, and we praise you.
   (Genuflect)

All: Because by your holy cross you have saved the world.
   (Stand)

Reader: When it was already evening, since it was the day of preparation, the day before the sabbath, Joseph of Arimathea, a distinguished member of the council, who was himself awaiting the kingdom of God... courageously went to Pilate and asked for the body of Jesus. Pilate was amazed that he was already dead. He summoned the centurion and asked him if Jesus had already died. And when he learned of it from the centurion, he gave the body to Joseph. Having bought a linen cloth, he took him down, wrapped him in the linen cloth and laid him in a tomb that had been hewn out of the rock. Then he rolled a stone against the entrance to the tomb.

Mark 15:42-46

   (Kneel)

Leader: Starting on Good Friday, the Church enters into a brief period of silent grief, a time of mourning that looks with hope to the joy of the resurrection that will be proclaimed and celebrated at the Easter Vigil. We grieve in much the same way when someone we love dies. There are tears and sorrow, of course, but rays of hope and belief in a later reunion bring us comfort, understanding, and strength.

All: My soul rests in God alone,
   from whom comes my salvation.
   God alone is my rock and salvation,
   my fortress; I shall never fall....
   My soul, be at rest in God alone,
   from whom comes my hope.

Psalm 62:2-3,6

(Stand)

All sing:

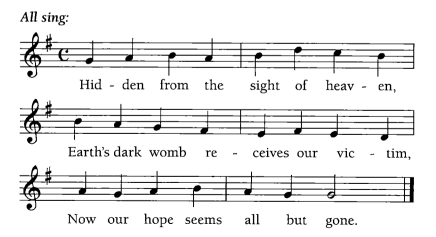

Hid – den from the sight of heav – en,

Earth's dark womb re – ceives our vic – tim,

Now our hope seems all but gone.

The Fifteenth Station

Jesus Rises From the Dead

Leader: We adore you, O Christ, and we praise you.
(Genuflect)

All: Because by your holy cross you have saved the world.
(Stand)

Reader: When the sabbath was over, Mary Magdalene, Mary, the mother of James, and Salome bought spices so that they might go and anoint him. Very early when the sun had risen, on the first day of the week, they came to the tomb. They were saying to one another, "Who will roll back the stone for us from the entrance to the tomb?" When they looked up, they saw that the stone had been rolled back; it was very large. On entering the tomb they saw a young man sitting on the right side, clothed in a white robe, and they were utterly amazed. He said to them, "Do not be amazed! You seek Jesus of Nazareth, the crucified. He has been raised; he is not here. Behold, the place where they laid him."

Mark 16:1-6

(Remain standing)

Leader: After the cross comes the crown. After three days of mourning and waiting, the Church celebrates Jesus' Resurrection. He is victorious. The Light of the World has conquered darkness. The Way, the Truth, and the Life has overcome death. We hear Jesus' words, "Peace be with you." We feel joy in our hearts. We sing again that acclamation of praise, "Alleluia."

His triumph is ours as well. On Easter Sunday, and in the many other Easters of our lives, we rise above our failures, our burdens, and our struggles. We, too, emerge victorious. Throughout our own Good Fridays, the risen Lord is by our side, pledging that we, too, will rise again, both here on earth and hereafter, in the life yet to come.

All: Praise the LORD, my soul;
I will praise the LORD all my life,
sing praise to my God while I live....
The LORD sets prisoners free...
The LORD shall reign forever,
your God, Zion, through all generations!

Psalm 146:1b,2,7b,10a

All sing:

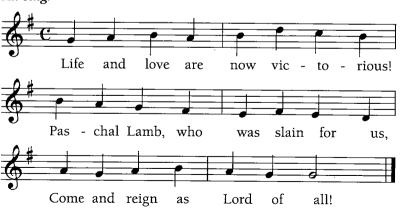

Life and love are now vic - to - rious!

Pas - chal Lamb, who was slain for us,

Come and reign as Lord of all!

Day By Day Through Lent
Reflections, Prayers, Practices
ISBN: 9780892-431946

Daily reflections based on the Gospel with a prayer and suggested practice for making the most of Lent.

The Essential Lenten Handbook
A Daily Companion
ISBN: 9780764-805677

The Essential Lenten Handbook provides everything readers need for a richer experience of the 40 days before Easter. Whether one wishes to follow a traditional program of Lenten devotions centered around prayer, a "modern" program that focuses on Scripture readings, a family model that brings loved ones together for a shared spiritual journey, or a unique devotional program, this all-in-one resource is an invaluable reference and the quintessential compact guidebook to all of the basic Lenten practices of Catholicism.

Seven Words of Jesus and Mary
Lessons on Cana and Calvary
FULTON SHEEN
ISBN: 9780764-807084

Analyzes the relation between the seven recorded words that Mary spoke in the Gospels and seven last words of her Son as He hung on the cross. Offers solace for the fears and dilemmas of today's Christian by interpreting the Gospel from the intertwined perspective of Mother and Son.

To order visit your local bookstore or call 800-325-9521 or visit us at www.liguori.org